$200

HAS THE DEMOCRATIC PARTY BECOME SOCIALIST?

A PRIMER ON SOCIALISM FOR THE 2020 ELECTION

HAS THE DEMOCRATIC PARTY BECOME SOCIALIST?

A PRIMER ON SOCIALISM FOR THE 2020 ELECTION

MERRILL RING

Preface

This short book is intended to be politically useful in the 2020 elections.

Being useful means that it is not a scholarly work – it is not to be comprehensive, saying everything that could be said (and at other times and places should be said.) It is to be short enough to show at least the outlines of the issues that will arise about socialism during the election campaign.

It is, with its limited aim, intended to be an explanation of what socialism is and how socialism is (or is not) playing a role in debates and discussions within the Democratic Party and between Democrats. It is not an attempt to defend socialism or to take a position on the question of whether socialism is a better form of economy than what we now have.

Given widespread current misconceptions – which exist in virulent form among conservatives but are even present among progressives and liberals (in the early Democratic debates both Delaney and Hickenlooper charged fellow Democratic candidates with advocating socialist programs) - in American political life about what socialism is and who is a socialist, the aim of explaining matters must take the form of correcting those misconceptions.

I think that the possibility of converting the American economy to socialism needs to be a major theme in our political discourse. To call for Americans to take socialism seriously, as a live possibility, is not the same as defending that kind of economic organization. The explanation, even in the limited form offered here, must precede arguing for or against.

By the way, to get the suspense eliminated, the short answer to the question in the title of this work is (probably following a belly laugh) is 'Of course not'. Anyone who knows political thought, both everyman's and specialist, in this country would find it astonishing that anyone could imagine that the Democrats are now (and have ever been) a socialist party. (That of course does not say anything about the dim future.) There is, of course, a longer answer: 'Don't try to answer the question now – wait until you've read the entire book.'

Thanks

I must deeply thank Tad Beckman for his construction of the excellent cover for this book. I merely asked for advice - he leaped into the project wholeheartedly.

Thanks for comments and suggestions are also due Nancy McFarland, Bob Nelson, Ted Panzer and Andy Winnick. I also borrowed an idea from Parkes Riley.

Finally, any money that comes to me from the sale of this book, either in its paperback or e-book form, will be donated to the Jerry Voorhis Democratic Club of Claremont and The American Institute for Progressive Democracy.

HAS THE DEMOCRATIC PARTY BECOME SOCIALIST?

A PRIMER ON SOCIALISM FOR THE 2020 ELECTION

Socialism, Republicans and the 2020 Election

Donald J. Trump is in all probability going to be the Republican nominee for President in the 2020 election - that will be so unless he is in jail or is otherwise forced from office (and the spending his time tweeting from Mar-a-Lago or his Moscow penthouse - encouraging a revolution to return him to power.)

Both Trump and the Republican Party will be (and even now are) running on the theme that the Democratic Party, whether its nominee is a progressive or a centrist, is a party of socialists.

Consider the t-shirt that Mitch McConnell is pushing, the Grim Reaper t-shirt. On the back it says "So think of me as the Grim Reaper who is going to make sure that socialism doesn't land on the President's desk"; the front shows a tombstone with 'Socialism' chiseled on it. Or this news report: "The Trump campaign is flying a 4,800 square-foot aerial banner above the Democratic debate site in Houston on Thursday. The campaign is also running full-page ads in the area's top newspapers – both read 'Socialism will kill Houston's economy. Vote Trump 2020'."

That Republican strategy means it is time for we progressives to freshen up on the topic of socialism. This primer is meant to be a brief guide to the topic and to provide a way to respond to the right-wing on the topic of socialism. But it isn't for progressives only - it is to be hoped that others will read it and learn. What needs to be learned is what socialism is, and the truth about the matter is completely contrary to what the Republicans and the Grim Reaper imply that it is.

There are some essential background points to be mentioned.

(1) As this work is an attempt to clear up misconceptions and to keep our terminology straight, it must be noticed right at the beginning that all of the

terminology involved is very fluid. There are so many intellectual versions of socialism, versions that do not agree on many issues, that anyone who tries clarify must step on someone's toes or tongue). (Note: those who write in criticism of socialism are very likely to think that there is only one thing called by that name.) So just remember that when I say socialism involves such-and-such, not everyone who has written on the subject will agree.

(2) Moreover, it is not just the intellectual versions of socialism that are so various. Actual economic systems which might rightly be called socialist are also not alike. Both in time and space, socialist systems (and capitalist ones too) can have large differences, while still qualifying for the title of socialist (or capitalist).

(3) An obvious assumption will be made here: it is capitalism that is the

economic system that socialism aims to replace.

(4) This primer is not intended to be a defense of socialism. Rather, what is said here will be a *preliminary* to either defense or criticism. This work is an attempt to explain the notion of socialism in face of massive confusions on the part of right-wing critics of it, but also, sadly enough, on the part of progressive thinkers and progressive political actors.

(5) It is intended that this primer be open-ended - there is no fixed number of items that I intend to discuss here. One thing leads to another. So, do not look for The End: that will come sometime, but as I start, it is not certain when that will be.

Socialism as Bogeyman

The resurgence of public discussions of socialism, the willingness of a *few* Democratic political figures to call themselves socialists, and polls showing that young adults say that they regard socialism more highly than capitalism, have led to a right-wing freak-out. Conservatives (and libertarians) are flat-out afraid. Not that anything has happened: it is the mere public appearance of the bogeyman, the very use of the 'S' word in public, that has caused the anxiety.

My favorite expression of the fear, and the attempt to cause others to share in it, is a piece from an organization called The Media Research Center. The piece blames "the liberal media" for causing socialism to be looked at favorably in some circles. Now of course, it isn't the media that are responsible for the resurgence of socialist talk in American public life (although blaming the media does suit the organization's agenda). It is easier to blame the media than it is to point to the serious difficulties, e.g. massive and increasing inequality, the climatic endangerment of Earth, that is causing thoughtful young people to start to reconsider an alternative economic system. So, not wanting to look in that direction, another right-wing bogeyman (the MSM) is trotted out in explanation.

It is worth our time to read (and savor) what is passing for thought in right-wing circles about the matter of socialism. The organization mentioned above has this to say.

"Socialism is on the rise in America and it owes its newfound popularity to the nefarious efforts of the activist liberal press. They are selling radical socialism to America's young people, making young socialists into social media stars, and entrenching them in Congress. Why does it matter? The liberal media are force feeding their poisonous ideology to the American people. Socialism is a real danger to our democracy and the American way of life. By censoring conservative voices and using their platform to push their leftist extremism, they are putting our country at risk and

jeopardizing the futures of generations of Americans. <u>This is a threat we cannot ignore.</u>

"The Media Research Center is committed to combating liberal bias in the media and standing up for conservative values. We know what is truly at stake and understand that no other organization has the experience or the expertise to fight this battle. If the leftist media are left to their own devices, socialism will become a permanent fixture in America, taxes will soar, the ridiculous Green New Deal will bankrupt our country, and open borders will compromise America's security. But we can't do it on our own. <u>We need patriotic Americans like you</u> in order to make the greatest possible impact. Our Grassroots Army is the best and most effective way for ordinary citizens to stand up for American values and take action against the radical leftist media and their socialist agenda."

So, socialism is a "poisonous ideology", it is a "danger" to "democracy", it is a danger to "the American way of life", it is un-American requiring real Americans ("patriots") to "battle" it, it is "leftist extremism", it poses a terrifying risk to the country, it "jeopardizes the future of generations of Americans", it is "a threat", it is an attack on "conservative values", "taxes will soar", it is the "agenda" behind the Green New Deal which is a "ridiculous" program that will "bankrupt" the country.

Notice that nothing specific about what socialism is gets mentioned there. It is as though the nature of socialism is well-known. Socialism is just something deeply scary no matter what it is, something that must be fought to the end. The prospect sketched makes socialism to be like something in a horror movie, some unknown alien force invading the country, threatening life as we know it.

What we need to do is to see what, behind the horror story, the right thinks socialism is, and then see what it actually is in order to start a rational discussion of what it would be for the United States to become a socialist country.

Three Typical Right-wing Assumptions About Socialism

At a slightly deeper level than the horror, there are two assumptions about the nature of socialism that must be noted and confronted at the beginning of this expose.

What is spoken of as socialism by some conservatives is simply whatever someone on the left is for. That is, it is already assumed that Democrats, especially those left of center, are socialists and whatever they propose must be a socialist program. Of course, the party is not now and has not ever been a socialist party – that it is a socialist political party is an idea that genuine socialists would find quite astonishing and so can be dismissed out of hand.

An equally absurd idea, though one that is fairly rampant in ordinary right wing talk about socialism, is that socialism is about 'free stuff', that all it amounts to is giving stuff to people. That idea of what socialism is rests on the notion that the stuff is to be given away for no other reason than that it is a way of winning votes. The combination of ignorance and cynicism in this common view is mind-boggling but there is an audience for it out there.

A more sophisticated assumption is that socialism is any *government* action that is intended to help or support others, to aid citizens in distress, to give people a better life. For example, ever since its inception, Social Security has been talked of as socialism by the right, even though it is not. It is a way of providing for the welfare of older and disabled people.

That is not a specifically socialist idea at all, though of course socialists, along with others, including many liberal capitalists, support such a program.

However, there is something to that assumption. For surely, socialism is intended to provide a better life for citizens. Of course, that intention does not distinguish socialism from other projects for public assistance to people. What is to be noticed is that the conservative here is holding a view that is best expressed by Ayn Rand: we must be concerned only with ourselves: any concern with the well-being of others is irrational and immoral. The name 'socialism' gets appropriated to stand for the opposite of the Randian view: any concern with the well-being of others is socialist. That mish-mash is a way of papering over very important distinctions.

(By the way, the discussion above focused only on individuals. Is government assistance to organizations also socialism? Are subsidies or tax breaks to industries or to religious organizations also socialist? If the assumption that any help *government* gives is socialist, then surely public monies given, or not required to be paid, is socialism. If that is so, we have many more socialist enterprises in this country than are usually noticed!)

Capitalism in the Constitution

When the right-wing critic of socialism starts claiming that socialism is un-American, that it is contrary to what America is, often they are treating the matter as a constitutional issue. This line of opposition to socialism tends to assume that we have a capitalist economic system in this country *because* that is what the Constitution requires. So, socialism is constitutionally un-American.

In fact, the U.S. Constitution does not forbid socialism nor does it require capitalism.

In the first place, the Constitution is a *political* document. It was not intended to address the economic organization of the country that it was founding. Even more, while the founders knew a lot about the history of political life, they were not nearly so knowledgeable about economic matters. The first theoretical account of capitalism (Adam Smith's *The Wealth of Nations* published in 1776) had only recently become available to some of them. Their earliest economic debates had to do with the limited issues of tariffs and taxes, not with the overall organization of an economy.

Moreover, while the Constitution is roughly contemporaneous with the origins of a capitalist economy, it was written about 50 years before the 19th century critiques of capitalism that were the origin of the socialist tradition.

Though conservative American defenders of capitalism may find bits and pieces of possible arguments in favor of that economic system in or implied by the Constitution, those are but scraps; one can equally find scraps that would function in a defense of a socialist America.

Politics and Economics
Since the Constitution does not address the question of what economic system the U.S. shall have, it follows that we citizens have a choice under that constitution as to how we shall organize our economic life. Given that we conduct our political life by voting on representatives and on issues, it is quite possible for us to vote to replace our historically dominant system, that of capitalism, with some socialist system.

Two points: first, it is our political will that, in the end, determines how our economy is organized and, second, it is not only by revolution that a socialist economy comes to be (see Great Britain in the post-WWII years where socialism was instituted by legislation).

The first point runs counter to a major thesis, derived from Karl Marx, that everything else in a country is determined by - and 'determined' is the correct word - the underlying economy. Politics is a superstructure, shaped entirely by the nature of the economy. The socialism being considered here does not accept that relationship – how our economy is structured can be settled by our political will, even if that requires democratic battling against the economic, and thus political, powers that be.

Given that we can make fundamental changes in the economy by choice, there are different ways of doing that. One is by revolution, another by, say, choices expressed at the ballot box. Socialism, as understood by those in the current public eye, is not to be achieved by force. To achieve a new kind of economy will surely involve massive actions outside the ballot box (demonstrations, strikes) but that is not the same thing as attempting to overthrow the existing government by force.

Socialism as Un-American (1)

To follow up on the theme of the bogeyman, the idea that socialism is not American and must therefore be kept at bay in this country, it is necessary to point out that there is a long socialist tradition in the U.S. (Probably the most readable account of that is John Nichols' *The "S" Word.*) Since telling the story of that history is not relevant here, let me make one small but revealing point.

One of the chief pieces of Americanism, something that we all learned as children - as we were required to recite it every day in school - is the Pledge of Allegiance. "I pledge allegiance to the flag of the United States of America and to ...."

Who wrote the Pledge? The author was Francis Bellamy. And who was Bellamy? He was a Christian Socialist minister. In other words, something that we all share as Americans, something at the heart of being a citizen of this country, **was created by a Socialist!**

Bellamy was important in the Christian Socialist movement, a significant feature of the 19th century political landscape in the U.S. In fact, he was a founder of the Society of Christian Socialists. Since so many of those who so strongly support capitalism today are also Christians, it is important to realize the Bellamy was not only a socialist but a Christian, so committed to his religion that he was a minister, Baptist no less. One feature of his religious teaching was that Jesus was a socialist. So, let us hear no more of the idea that being a socialist is un-American - nor of the idea that Christians are necessarily capitalists.

Socialism as Un-American (2)

But, someone will object at the point, even if capitalism is not enshrined in the Constitution, the country has had a capitalist economy forever and that makes us by our very nature capitalist. To even think of fundamentally changing our economic system is therefore to be un-American.

Let me not quibble and so grant that the country has had a predominantly (but not completely as we shall see) capitalist organization of its economy for much of its history.

However, it was the increasing hold that capitalism had on our economy in the 19th century and the increasing realization of its harsh realities, that produced an increasing opposition, even violent opposition, to capitalism in this country, just as there was in Europe. While most of the nation's energy in the 19th century was directed toward the slavery that was the basis of the southern economy (and that has shaped our entire history, economic and otherwise), it was only with the end of slavery and the consequent victory of an industrial economy that opposition to our existing economic system in general began.

Those who would identify America with capitalism simply are ignorant of how long and how extensive the criticism of capitalism and, alongside that criticism, activist opposition to it, have been. In this country there is a huge chunk of American history that has been ignored (covered up?) since the end of WWII. The aim has been to maintain a contrast between this country and communism as practiced in the Soviet Union - the U.S. is pure and capitalist while the Soviet Union is (was) bad and communist. Therefore, on the current orthodox view there cannot have been any anti-capitalism and so no socialist advocates here except for traitors.

While everyone learns something (though not enough) of the opposition to slavery, both intellectual opposition and activism, we are given a blah and benign picture of our history with respect to capitalism. Perhaps with the return of public discussion of socialism, our textbooks and our reading in general will come to exhibit the extensive historical conflict about our economic system.

Democracy

The socialism that has become a topic of public argument today is Democratic Socialism. The people in public office who declare themselves socialists always preface that affiliation with 'Democratic'. That qualification is very rarely commented upon by their critics: they hear the 'socialist' word and their fear erases the adjective.

Why does, say, Bernie Sanders but also young people, elected officials and others, always say that their socialism is democratic? There are two reasons.

The reference to democracy is intended in the first place, to contrast the socialism they are advocating with an alternative socialist tradition that thinks that the only way socialism can be become the economic organization of a country is by revolution - by over-throwing by force the existing government and it capitalist base. The current socialists are trying to inform the American public that they want socialism to prevail through normal democratic practices - which include demonstrations, marches, strikes, etc. - namely, by convincing people, voters, that capitalism needs to be replaced by a socialist economy and then winning not only public opinion battles but also elections.

There is a very long tradition, both in Europe and here, of socialists being significant defenders of democratic government.

The second reason the word 'Democratic' is prefaced to 'Socialist' leads to the heart of what socialism is. For the aim of socialism is to increase the range of democracy by expanding the range of democratic practices. A socialist economic system is to be understood as, and advocated for, because it *is the means to economic democracy, democracy extended from the political system to the economy.*

Without specifying further what economic democracy is, it must now be pointed out that the right-wing charge that instituting socialism in this country would be the death of democracy is wildly mistaken. In fact, the aim of democratic socialism is precisely the opposite, to bring about by democratic means a massive extension of the arena of democracy.

To satisfactorily say what economic democracy is requires, at least, addressing the central question of this primer.

What is Socialism?

The major purpose of this pamphlet is to clear up large confusions about what socialism is. Critics of it assume that it is one single ideology and that that set of ideas can be captured in a single formula. However, there are variants of socialism, in both theory and practice. And that leads to an important issue.

How Not to Answer the Question

When we are talking of economic systems, there are two different issues that must be kept in mind and distinguished.

On the one hand, to talk of, say, socialism, is to talk of a certain kind of economic system as an intellectual construct, an ideology, a system of ideas and ideals. On the other hand, talk of socialism (or any other economic system) can be about the existence of a certain kind of economic system in some particular country at some specific time, a creation almost certainly with an allegiance to a specific set of ideas.

What is quite mistaken, but indulged in almost all the time by right-wing critics of socialism, is a conflation of the two matters: socialism - the intellectual construct - cannot be criticized by directing attention to the way it was practiced in some particular country, say England: *unless*, that is, it is shown that the set of features of the socialism as practiced in country X is a necessary consequence of socialist ideas.

The reason is that how socialism (or capitalism or ...) is practiced in such and such a place and at a certain time is not simply a function of the system of ideas, but also is how that set of ideas is implemented in that specific place with its own history, its own social, political and intellectual culture, the time and people who are establishing the system and those who are living lives in the local economy. So, when American critics of capitalism fault capitalism, they may be faulting it as embodying certain necessary features contained in the set of ideas called 'capitalism' or they may be responding only to features of the system as practiced in this country. So too for socialism: critics must be very careful to distinguish whether it is socialism *per se* they are criticizing or whether it is how it operates in a particular place and at a particular time.

It is quite acceptable to point to the embodiment of, say socialism, in such and such a time and/or place as *examples* of how the doctrine has been realized then and there. How it functioned in that time and place has to do not only with the ideas, but with the circumstances in which those ideas were being put into practice.

That crucial distinction is so very often overlooked by critics of socialism. They importantly are not careful about which project they are engaged in. Especially they are guilty of going on and on about the economic evils of the Soviet Union as though the Soviet economy was, in the first place, a socialist system in the sense of socialism relevant to, say, the 2020 election and, in the second place, as though there is no difference between the socialist ideas and the features of Russia that housed that particular system. (Sometimes Cuba or Venezuela is inserted into the discussion instead of the Soviet Union.)

That assimilation of projects is so common among right-wing commentators that we on the left need to be constantly prepared to combat it.

It should be noticed that those who collapse the ideology and the practice of socialism in a certain time and place and then criticize the ideology on what happened then and there, always assume that those who are socialists are quite incapable of learning from what has happened in that time and place. Socialism failed in place X, so it is inevitable that it will fail the next time it is tried.

But of course, socialists aren't stupid and unable to learn. Many of the changes in socialist thought have come about because it was recognized that, trying to do such-and-such under such-and-such conditions won't work and so shouldn't be tried again. If a certain experiment in socialism hasn't worked, then it is necessary to understand why it failed and to set about not repeating the past.

The Anti-Capitalist Tradition: Terminology

I know that talk of terminology is often boring, but nonetheless it is equally often important. Attention to terminology is quite important in understanding how to address issues concerning socialism.

In the following sections I will be talking of the Anti-Capitalism Tradition. That is unusual. Most writers, both supporters and opponents of socialism, talk of the Socialist Tradition. That change of terminology is quite important. For what talking in the standard way (about the Socialist Tradition at this point in the discussion) does is to encourage critics of socialism to ignore the differences between distinct traditions within anti-capitalism. And so socialism is said to involve such-and-such when it is only one of the different anti-capitalism positions.

I shall be distinguishing and discussing three different solutions to the problems of capitalism, solutions that were created in the 19th century and which persist today. Social democracy, socialism and communism are all distinct ideas but they all did emerge from the same 19th century background. They are and have been partners in the opposition to capitalism, in the anti-capitalist movement.

What makes matters confusing is that in the beginning all the anti-capitalists thought of themselves as belonging together as socialists. Only as positions became clarified over time did it become possible to sort out three major positions within anti-capitalism and to assign different names to them. One of the names, socialism, was the remainder of the name originally applied to the entire movement. As critics love to argue on the basis of that original grouping and to resist differentiation of what are different ideas about how to solve the ills of capitalism, it is best to rename the whole historical grouping - and so it is important to talk of anti-capitalism.

The Anti-Capitalism Tradition: Criticism of Capitalism

Writers on the right tend to talk as if anti-capitalism just popped into someone's head one fine morning: 'Wow, let's have the government take over and operate our economy.'

Socialism cannot be understood unless it is first situated in both a particular historical setting and a broad intellectual current. The historical setting is of course the rise and expansion of capitalism, especially the developments following the industrial revolution (which began about 1760).

As the 19th century went on, capitalism evolved and spread geographically. With those developments, the consequences of capitalism (good and bad) became more and more clear. For those who were deeply bothered by the harm the new economy was causing, it was necessary not only to protest it, but to analyze just what it is about a capitalist economy that causes extensive misery as well as an abundance of goods. And then, and only then, it became possible to articulate what an alternative economic system would be that would end the harms produced by capitalism. (Remember that the protesting of economic conditions had been going on roughly forever - the critique of capitalism went hand in hand with a new stage in the protest tradition.)

It must also be pointed out here, that there also developed a strong tradition defending capitalism, arguing that it was a magnificent human invention and was, and would be, making the world a better place. The tradition became known as (classical) liberalism. Its opponents early on were the conservative defenders of the old ways, the landed aristocracy. Only as that form of economic, political and social life faded away, did the rising new anti-capitalism become the object of attention on the part of proponents of capitalism. The various new critiques and programs then became the enemy of the liberal tradition.

What was, and is, the criticism of capitalist economic systems that led to solutions, one of which is socialism? It is impossible to set that out fully here so all I shall try to do is present a version that captures (I think) the chief points.

Capitalism is a system that rests upon the productive resources of a country being owned privately and being used to make profits for those owners. Profits are the extra money remaining from sales after operating expenses and re-investment savings are deducted from income. Those profits belong to the owners (the capitalists) and are increases in their wealth. All decisions about the operation of the firm are the owner's to make and they will be made with an eye only to the profit to be made. Since a business requires many more people than the owner in order to create the product - workers in the classic terminology - there must be a pool of such people available (a much larger group than that of the capitalists). They are paid a wage for working and producing: they have no responsibility for any of the operational decisions. There comes to be a great disparity between the wealth of the owners (derived from profits) and that of those who work for them. That inequality is a basic feature of a capitalist economy. And inequality in wealth leads to even further inequality in power than already exists in the owner-worker relation.

The above description of the analysis of capitalism by its historical critics omits something extremely important: it is anti-septic, it contains no mention of the misery level of the workers, of the large majority of the population, when classical capitalism had no serious activist or intellectual opposition. The origins of anti-capitalism, both as activism and as critique, are not intelligible without realizing that it was the huge contrast between the wealth and power of the few compared to the suffering of the many that led people to oppose capitalism.

Digression: Markets

I have intentionally omitted reference to markets in the above account of capitalism, although talking of markets (especially 'free' ones) is a very typical way of saying what capitalism is. So, I must say something about the omission and its consequences.

It strikes me as a mistake to treat 'market economy' as a synonym for 'capitalism'. While markets are a central feature of your standard capitalist economy, that does not mean that they are by definition constitutive of capitalism.

If the capitalists, the owners of the businesses in a capitalist economy, had their way, there would be no markets in which they compete to sell their goods. Each business would love to have a monopoly - they and only they would be the supplier of good X to consumers. Only theorists and consumers like markets, i.e. competition. If you include the notion of a market in a definition of capitalism, that inclination by the very owners of enterprises in a capitalist economy is hidden.

A further reason: once markets are identified with capitalism, the idea of market socialism becomes impossible - but there are advocates of just such an economic system, one in which non-private/non-profit driven enterprises compete (in some ways) for sales of their goods.

However, it also needs to be recognized that while there have been markets in even ancient economies - goods produced that are not intended for household consumption are sold in markets - there is something quite different in a capitalist economy, one in which there is competition. There the entire product is produced for a market - and competition is, for both owners and workers, a major, sometimes overwhelming, feature of daily life.

There is no simple way of either including the notion of markets into an account of what capitalism is or of excluding it from the discussion. Just be wary of those who would insist that it is the very essence of capitalism (especially when they toss in the adjective 'free') for the economic system to be a market economy. For that evades the fact that it is private ownership, which is profit-driven and which requires wage labor, that is at the heart of the anti-capitalist criticism.

The Anti-Capitalist Tradition: Solutions

From the turmoil, both in the streets and in intellectual circles, of the 19th century anti-capitalist movement, there came to be several different solutions for how to deal with the new economic system of capitalism. Some of those I will be skipping over in this primer since the aim is to talk about current politics.

Those solutions I shall not be examining here are, first, what Marx called Utopian Socialism, anti-capitalist solutions developed by Charles Fourier and Robert Owen. There was also, at the time, a significant Anarchist view of what to do about capitalism (and the state). None of those varieties figure importantly in current political conversations, so I will not be talking further of them.

The three sets of ideas that emerged from the earlier debates and acts and which are the major components of today's anti-capitalism debates are Social Democracy, Socialism and Communism. Once again, the reader needs to be reminded that the terminology, both historical and often contemporary, is much messier than I am proposing here: but for our current political needs and the purposes of this work, it is important to draw sharp distinctions.

To distinguish the three major branches of anti-capitalism, let me employ a scheme produced by a friend, a professor of politics. Since it omits something of great importance to answering the question What is Socialism?, I will *not* be taking it as providing a *definition* of any of the three positions. That will become clear as we proceed. So what follows is a way of setting out what are, for our present political purposes, three different varieties of anti-capitalist economic systems.

(1). Social Democracy: Capitalism remains but is regulated by the state, sometimes highly regulated.

(2). Socialism: Capitalism vanishes for the major enterprises in the economy, ownership of which is typically transferred to the state. (Please notice the "typically" – the socialist tradition has come to recognized that non-state owned enterprises can be socialist (more on that later.))

(3). Communism: All businesses are state owned.

Economic Democracy

To complete this broad account of the anti-capitalism solutions to the problems of capitalism, it is now necessary to re-introduce the notion of economic democracy.

I said earlier that the charge against socialism of being anti-democratic gets matters completely backward because the aim of all the major historical solutions that arose out of the anti-capitalist critique is to extend the practice of democracy into the economic system.

Democracy is a political system based on the idea that all citizens are equal and so should have an equal say in the governance of the country. But, the argument goes, since capitalist firms are not democratic entities - capitalist enterprises are the property of a person or group entitled to make all decisions no matter how those decisions affect others (the workers, the community, the country) - there is a central failing in any country that professes to be democratic and yet allows capitalism to hold sway in the productive life of its citizens. Consequently, in the pursuit of equality and democracy, those firms at the center of the economy must also be brought under democratic control.

In the case of socialism, it is not public ownership of major sections of the economy that is sought for its own sake: the aim is to make them democratic institutions by taking the power away from private owners. That is why any definition of socialism that focuses only on the public ownership fails - it omits the reason for the transfer of ownership.

Moreover, it is possible to have public ownership without any (serious) attempt to have the enterprise operated democratically: in the United States neither the Tennessee Valley Authority (TVA) nor the Veterans Administration health care system (VA) are subject to control by the people who work there nor by the community. They are thus incompletely socialized enterprises (as was the entire Soviet economy).

Communism

The third of those major sets of ideas that derived from 19th century objections to capitalism was communism. For our purposes, communism is the idea that government ought to own and operate *every* enterprise in the economy - not just the huge major players but even retail businesses of all sorts, the mom and pop store on the corner. In economic terms, communism is a command economy where every economic decision is made by the government.

Communism certainly has a bad rap because it was institutionalized in Russia (which became the Soviet Union or more fully, showing its ancestry, the Union of Soviet *Socialist* Republics). Its existence there was a grim period in the history of Europe, both for Russians and for the West (even the entire world). Its failure in the USSR was to be expected historically: communism in the Soviet Union became the governing economic (and political) system through non-democratic means in a country just a short step away from its feudal past and with no tradition of democracy or of capitalism.

As a result, only half of the anti-capitalist program could be brought about in the Soviet Union: democracy and equality were impossible there. All that could and would be done was to have the state own and operate every piece of the economy. What the USSR became was not socialism (and not even communism as it can be imagined) but a system of *state capitalism*. A small group of people made all the decisions about economic (and political) life - the overwhelming number of ordinary people had as little economic power as ordinary people did in the early days of capitalism.

For our purposes, however, since we are focusing on communism as an economic system, the important point is that it involves a command economy and that requires that the state be capable of making every economic judgment. In the complex contemporary world, especially in a country which is not, say, the size of Monaco, such a system simply cannot function well enough to be a serious possibility. And so I shall be dropping communism as a candidate for what kind of economy the United States ought to have.

Anti-Capitalist Economies and Welfare

There are then (for our purposes) two alternative forms of non-capitalist economy (each with many variations) that have possible application to the United States at the present time: Social Democracy and Socialism. I will be looking into each.

First, however, it is necessary to introduce another topic - that of welfare provisions. In the United States, welfare is about such things as Social Security, unemployment benefits, disability, health insurance (the ACA). Public education can be counted here also.

The very mention of those welfare provisions is likely to set the conservative off screaming of socialism (as I pointed out earlier, Social Security from its inception has been treated by right wing thinkers as a socialist scheme).

But those programs are not socialism - neither do they belong to the second kind of non-capitalist economy being considered here, namely social democracy. I do not know enough about the practice of communism in the Soviet bloc to know whether any similar programs were in existence there - though I suspect that some were. The point is that a system of welfare, covering programs such as those mentioned above, is a constituent of anti-capitalist economies and is not specific to any particular form of those.

In fact, that account is too narrow. The original welfare state was Otto von Bismarck's Germany in the late 19th century and he, thorough conservative that he was, instituted welfare programs, including universal health care. And the reason that he did it, correctly distinguishing between such programs and non-capitalist economic systems, was precisely to block a change in economy from capitalism to something else (which he broadly labelled 'socialism').

When we focus on what the variations in anti-capitalism are, it must not be forgotten that all of them hold that a system of welfare must be included for the well-being of people living in such economies (though the precise reasons for those may well vary from one kind of system to the other).

Social Democracy

As noted in the very brief account of social democracy above, it retains capitalist ownership of (most) economic enterprises, while, in the interests of lessening the great inequalities of unregulated capitalism, it offers the idea of regulating for the public good the capitalist economic system.

In social democracies, there are two quite different systems employed to soften the ill effects of completely free enterprise. There is a set of rules designed to protect those not capable of fully functioning in a capitalist economy. These are the welfare state rules: unemployment compensation, Social Security, Medicare, aid to the poor and disabled, etc.

But the second set of social democratic rules is the imposition of regulations on various features of capitalist economic activity. In the United States, think of child labor laws or laws governing worker compensation or laws demanding that milk not be mixed with chalk, even rules eliminating entire possible enterprises (say payday lending or gun-slinging).

Note: it may be difficult to sort any particular piece of legislation into one or the other of those categories. And there may be other rules designed to prevent those with much wealth from having too great an influence in democratic politics.

While the Scandinavian countries are the chief practitioners of social democracy, it is obvious that we in the United States have succeeded in hugely various ways and to hugely various degrees in eliminating the greatest excesses of unrestrained capitalism by social democratic practices.

Should we then be called a Social Democratic country? Surely not, for two reasons. First, there are so many features of capitalism that are unregulated here that it would be a mistake to think that we have earned the title of Social Democracy - think for instance of the great income (and consequent wealth) disparity between the compensation of CEO's of corporations and the wage compensation of workers. The second reason that we do not bear the title is that the entire ethos of our economic practice is capitalist: we do not proclaim ourselves to be a social democracy and since we do not think of ourselves as such we do not as a matter of public policy take major steps toward decreasing inequality.

Much of the time, critics fail to distinguish Social Democracy and Socialism as economic systems. Defenders of capitalism dream of the old days when there were no public restraints on the operation of a privately-owned enterprise and so they sloppily ignore any differences between ways of dealing with the faults of capitalism.

Classical Socialism
Socialism, classical socialism, is one of the three major anti-capitalism ideologies that came out of the ferment of the 19th century. It should be clear by

now that if one wants something by way of a definition, it would consist of two parts.

One piece of an account of what socialism is, and this is the item that is usually mentioned, is the idea that the state should own and operate the major industries. Unlike communism, it does not hold that every business should be owned by the state: it is only those industries or businesses that so dominate the economic life of a particular nation the they cannot safely be left in private hands. This matter is usually put as the idea that the state shall own the means of production. Of course, what those industries are is subject to change from nation to nation and from time to time.

For instance, when Great Britain nationalized its basic industries after World War II, what was included were the coal industry, the banking system, the health industry, electricity production, railroads and other transportation systems, gas supply, the iron and steel industries. If the United States were to indulge in a comparable nationalization, it is an interesting exercise to try to work out what would be included. (Though they may not fit easily under the heading of 'means of production', would, say, Amazon and Google, be included in a nationalization scheme? They are after all major players in today's economy.)

The socialist argument that the state should acquire the basic and dominant industries is based on the analysis of the ills of society under capitalism. The chief objection is that being privately owned takes only private good into account: the aim of a capitalist firm is to make a profit no matter what the effects of striving to achieve that aim are on the people employed by the firm, on its customers, on the community and the nation. (We would today also importantly include the effects on the environment.). By making the industry public and eliminating the profit motive, an economy with the major industries put into public ownership would take the interest of all the stakeholders into account.

And so we come to the second of the constituent features of socialism: what I have called economic democracy. While it is popular to think of socialism as involving only public ownership of basic industries, that is quite mistaken. For the entire project is to produce an extension of democracy into the economic sphere. In a full, mature, socialist system, enterprises are to be operated by and for the public good and to be operated in a democratic manner.

It is of course possible to have an enterprise which satisfies the first of the two components of socialism, the public ownership part. Obviously, the cousin of socialism, the communist economy of the Soviet Union, failed to even try to satisfy that second requirement. Here in the

United States, the Tennessee Valley Authority (among others) is publicly owned and operated though it is not known to me how far they satisfy the economic democracy requirement.

The American Economy Today

If we look at the American economy in light of the above discussions of various economic systems, it is beyond any question that we are living in a capitalist economy. There is no point to continuing on that theme.

But it is not the form of capitalism that was being practiced without organized hindrance in its early days. While its major competitor (communism) has in practical terms, and largely in theoretical terms, ceased be a possibility for the country, we have made significant progress in blocking the horrible practices that were a product of unchecked capitalism - though that condition is still the dream of so very many leaders of today's capitalism, both leaders in thought and leaders in the production of goods and services. Free market, free enterprise is their recurring call. (Though it may be doubted that those who argue in favor of such a condition really understand what would be the consequences of a return to capitalism's rip-roaring early days.)

We have, by laws, rules and regulations, succeeded in taming the many of the worst excesses of capitalism as it was originally practiced.

Some of what has been accepted (though not by so many on the right) is the existence of a welfare system, protecting those who are not prized by capitalist thought and practice.

And then there are all the restrictions placed upon the behavior of enterprises operating in the economy, rendering our system considerably less than a free market.

However, it would be absurd to think we have become a social democratic economy, that our economic system deserves that title. Capitalism has become much more humane with our social democratic practices, but how very much remains to be done to achieve the vision of the social democratic wing of the anti-capitalist tradition.

We have also come to have a less than pure capitalism by having adopted some very small measures of socialism - measures much smaller in scope and effect than our social democratic practices. Some economic actors are publicly owned. Of course, there are those public enterprises long ago achieved: for instance, fire departments, road systems, postal services (though there are ongoing attempts to have that revert to private for-profit ownership). But there are more recent additions to that (very incomplete) list. I have pointed out previously that the Tennessee Valley Authority is a socialist enterprise conducting business alongside private electrification corporations. And the Veterans Administration health care system is a socialist operation, i.e. owned by the state (as is the National Health Service in Britain).

Most of the socialist enterprises in the United States are not in federal hands, but owned and operated by various other levels of government: municipal water and power agencies as well as the local fire and police departments. There may somewhere be a book setting out how many and how various are the socialist enterprises in the country.

There is another set of non-capitalist organizations with a role in our economy. (The existence of these is one reason for not identifying capitalism with markets.). Do you belong to a credit union? Credit unions are not publicly owned but neither are they aimed at profit making. In New Mexico I receive my electricity from a co-operative, a customer owned non-profit form of economic activity. We also buy a significant portion of our groceries from a co-op. There are also worker co-ops: non-publicly owned businesses whose ownership is in the hands of the people who work there. I do not know the extent of worker co-ops in this country, though they are a significant feature of the Spanish economy. Somewhat differently, the Green Bay Packers football team is community owned: it is a non-profit entity which competes in the professional football market.

The U.S. thus has something of a mixed economy - a fact that conservatives tend to overlook when they criticize socialism. However, the capitalist owned for profit sector is far and away the dominant kind of productive activity in this country even if has been importantly restrained by social democratic rules and regulations. Our economy is a mixture of some socialist and non-capitalist enterprises operating in a market economy dominated by capitalism modestly constrained by social democratic rules and regulations.

Democratic Socialism

In the U.S. today, as we come up to the 2020 elections, the dominant version of socialism in the country is not Classical Socialism but Democratic Socialism.

Bernie Sanders, the political figure most closely identified with socialism in the public and especially the conservative mind, always refers to himself not as a socialist but as a democratic socialist. Other elected officials on the national scene, most prominently Alexandria Ocasio-Cortez (AOC), also call themselves not socialists but democratic socialists.

It would seem, then, to understand what is going on about socialism in this country today we should pay attention first to the adjective and not the noun, to the qualification 'democratic' and only think after that what they have in mind by referring to themselves as socialists.

These current socialists want to emphasize their democratic credentials. By their name they are showing that they want their program to be instituted democratically, not by, say, armed revolution. They are out to convince the country to vote for a program for which they stand and which they call a socialist program. Secondly, the use of the word 'democratic' in representing what they stand for is to make clear that a central aim of their socialism is the democratizing of both the basic features of the economy and of the work-place itself.

What about the socialism part? Does democratic socialism differ at all from Classical Socialism? Right-wing critics do not take the time to ask this: they hear the word 'socialism' and they fly into a tizzy rather than investigating what is actually being proposed. Let me begin by looking not at individuals but at the democratic socialist organization that has become the leader in American socialism.

Democratic Socialists of America

That organization which is central to today's democratic socialism is the Democratic Socialists of America.

I don't know who introduced the term 'democratic socialist', but the organization that bears that title was founded by Michael Harrington (and friends) in 1982. Harrington, you will recall, is the author of *The Other America* (1962), the book that inspired the War on Poverty of John F. Kennedy and Lyndon Johnson. (Those were the days, not so long ago, that American Presidents were influenced by socialists though, of course, they were not socialists: they just knew an important idea when they heard it.)

The DSA has become the largest socialist organization in the U.S. with much recent growth due to the signing up of lots of young people (which is what gives defenders of capitalism extreme fright). There are now prominent DSA members holding public office, notably Alexandria Ocasio-Cortez and Rashida Tlaib in Congress. Bernie Sanders, while a democratic socialist, is not a member.

However, the organization is composed of an extensive range of anti-capitalist organizations that hold a variety of positions - not just the socialism of its title. And very importantly included are social democrats, an anti-capitalist view which must be distinguished from socialism.

In fact, the DSA, in terms of what it *currently* supports, *is a social democratic organization*. It does not believe that capitalism is going away any time soon - consequently it chiefly works to encourage government regulations in order to make private, for profit, enterprises accountable to the public good. And that is exactly what social democracy is.

Of course, the DSA expects that in the long run, through democratic means, socialism will prevail as the economic system in this country. But that is a long-term goal, to be approached through increasing restraints on capitalist practices and urges.

Secondly, the reference in the name of the organization to socialism is a reversion to the old days when all anti-capitalists called themselves socialists, before the differentiation of distinct positions (communism, social democracy and classical socialism). The DSA might appropriately be named **the Democratic Anti-Capitalists of America,** for it is an anti-capitalist big tent organization.

The Constitution of the organization offers a set of broadly spelled out reasons why it is a socialist (i.e. anti-capitalist) organization.

"We are socialists because we reject an economic order based on private profit, alienated labor, gross inequalities of

wealth and power, discrimination based on race, sex, sexual orientation, gender expression, disability status, age, religion, and national origin, and brutality and violence in defense of the status quo." [Note: those rejections, possibly except the first, would equally be cited by all contemporary anti-capitalist positions. The explanation does not at all say what their specific solution to all those social ills would be in the long run, namely public ownership of the major economic actors.]

"We are socialists because we share a vision of a humane social order based on popular control of resources and production, economic planning, equitable distribution, feminism, racial equality and non-oppressive relationships. [Once again, this is a mixture of what tends toward the specific notion of socialism and what would be held by all contemporary anti-capitalists – and much of it would equally be cited even by liberals.]

"We are socialists because we are developing a concrete strategy for achieving that vision, for building a majority movement that will make democratic socialism a reality in American. We believe that such a strategy must acknowledge the class structure of American society and that this class structure means that there is a basic conflict of interest between those sectors with enormous economic power and the vast majority of the population." [Note: this is not a reason for being socialists but a statement of intent. And it is a clear expression that the plan for having a socialist economy in the U.S. is both long term and democratic.]

To complete this account of the DSA one must notice the following material from its web site.

"Social ownership could take many forms, such as worker-owned cooperatives of publicly owned enterprises managed by workers and consumer representatives.

[Note: I will talk more of this when I come to a later section on Economic Democracy.]

"Democratic socialists favor as much decentralization as possible. While the large concentrations of capital in industries such as energy and steel may necessitate some form of state ownership, many consumer-goods industries might be best run as cooperatives." [Note: the idea that socialists have only one program with fixed solutions is belied by passages such as this – there are various possibilities for structuring the post-capitalist economy. Publicly owned enterprises are not the end all and be all of democratic socialism.]

"Democratic socialists have long rejected the belief that the whole economy should be centrally planned. [Note: this is an explicit rejection of the common right-wing idea that socialism is identical with Soviet style communism, that it advocates a command economy.]

"While we believe that democratic planning can shape major social investments like mass transit, housing and energy, market mechanisms are needed to determine the demand for many consumer goods." [Note: markets will survive under a democratic socialist economy.]

The final lesson: While the right in the coming election will try to make you believe that the socialism they attribute to the Democratic Party is intent on having the state take control of much if not all of the economy as quickly as possible, if you read and think about what the major organization, the Democratic Socialists of America, advocates, you will notice that there is no call, much less a ringing call, for nationalization of *any* major feature of the current economy. Perhaps conversion of some industries and enterprises from private ownership to public ownership might be the best solution – but that will require public discussion and democratic agreement.

The conservative view needs to be challenged: What industries does your favorite socialist want to be taken from private hands and when? There is *no* evidence *whatsoever* that the Democratic Party will include in its platform for 2020 a call for nationalization of *any* industry.

Bernie Sanders and Socialism (I)

When conservatives call Democrats 'socialists', they have one of two things in mind. First, as talked about much earlier, any view that advocates care and concern for the economic well-being of others by public means is thought of by the right as socialist. For instance, along with Social Security, the Affordable Care Act is thought of as socialist by true blue defenders of capitalism. The general idea that working to achieve a better economic life, and thus a better life generally for people other than **oneself**, and the application of that view to specific programs such as Social Security or the ACA, is socialism is, of course, nonsense.

But there it is, enshrined in conservative public discourse, and it is not going away soon (despite the aims of this work).

Secondly, in today's political world, Bernie Sanders is always trotted out as the arch-socialist. In the media he is always identified as 'Bernie, self-described socialist'. No one has ever seen in political reportage 'Donald Trump, capitalist' or 'Elizabeth Warren, social democrat': it is only Sanders (well, sometimes these days so are AOC and Tlaib) who gets shoved into a named category, the model of a socialist political figure.

So, given Sanders' position in the public mind, looking more carefully into what he intends by calling himself a democratic socialist and into what he proposes, is important in coming to understand socialism today.

Remember: to be a member of the Democratic Socialists of America is not necessarily to be a socialist as that term is best understood. You cannot infer from membership in the organization whether someone (say AOC) is a socialist, though they most certainly are some form of anti-capitalist. Moreover, Bernie Sanders does not seem to have membership in the DSA - though bearing the same title, he is (as usual) a lone wolf.

Ok, what does this current paradigm of democratic socialism say of his political views? He has twice (in 2016 and more recently) explained what he thinks democratic socialism to be.

"Today in the second decade of the 21st century, we must take up the unfinished business of the New Deal and carry it to completion.... We must recognize that in the 21st century, in the wealthiest country in the history of the world, economic rights are human rights. That is what I mean by democratic socialism."

Sanders, when explaining what he advocates, harks back to FDR, who was not at all a socialist. In fact, Roosevelt's aim was to save capitalism. (Imagine conservatives praising FDR, as they should, for saving capitalism in the 1930's!) To save it required (requires?) a major transformation of the economy, to be rid of those features of American capitalism, and the social system that it supports, that placed it in imminent danger of being thrown overboard by the misery of the Great Depression. Sanders sees himself as working to complete the program of the New Deal.

His positive thesis is "economic rights are human rights" - that is at the heart of his democratic socialism.

I'm going to insert a reminder of how the thesis that we need economic rights expressed itself in FDR's New Deal. We can thereby get by that a better idea of what Bernie understands democratic socialism to be.

Economic Rights in the New Deal

It seems quite clear that Sanders is explicitly connecting his version of democratic socialism to what is often referred to as FDR'S "Second Bill of Rights" which was set out in his 1944 State of the Union address.

Remember that that address was given in the midst of World War II. FDR was both looking back at the state of the country prior to the war - and also looking forward to what the country needed to do after the war.   Also remember that in the 75 years since then, so many details of our economy have changed - ignore those out-of-date provisions in this first version of an Economic Bill of Rights.

January 11, 1944
It is our duty now to begin to lay the plans and determine the strategy for the winning of a lasting peace and the establishment of an American standard of living higher than ever before known. We cannot be content, no matter how high that general standard of living may be, if some fraction of our people — whether

*it be one-third or one-fifth or one-tenth —
is ill-fed, ill-clothed, ill-housed, and
insecure.*

*This Republic had its beginning, and
grew to its present strength, under the
protection of certain inalienable political
rights — among them the right of free
speech, free press, free worship, trial by
jury, freedom from unreasonable searches
and seizures. They were our rights to life
and liberty.*

*As our nation has grown in size and
stature, however — as our industrial
economy expanded — these political rights
proved inadequate to assure us equality in
the pursuit of happiness.*

*We have come to a clear realization
of the fact that true individual freedom
cannot exist without economic security and
independence. "Necessitous men are not
free men." People who are hungry and out
of a job are the stuff of which dictatorships
are made.*

In our day these economic truths have become accepted as self-evident. We have accepted, so to speak, a second Bill of Rights under which a new basis of security and prosperity can be established for all — regardless of station, race, or creed.

Among these are:

The right to a useful and remunerative job in the industries or shops or farms or mines of the nation;

The right to earn enough to provide adequate food and clothing and recreation; The right of every farmer to raise and sell his products at a return which will give him and his family a decent living;

The right of every businessman, large and small, to trade in an atmosphere of freedom from unfair competition and domination by monopolies at home or abroad;

The right of every family to a decent home;

The right to adequate medical care and the opportunity to achieve and enjoy good health;

The right to adequate protection from the economic fears of old age, sickness, accident, and unemployment;

The right to a good education.

All of these rights spell security. And after this war is won we must be prepared to move forward, in the implementation of these rights, to new goals of human happiness and well-being.

America's own rightful place in the world depends in large part upon how fully these and similar rights have been carried into practice for our citizens.

Sanders and Socialism (II)

What Bernie Sanders adds to FDR's Economic Bill of Rights – given that the world and our economy are not the same as they were in 1944 – is the idea that those rights are held by Americans because they are human beings. Now I will not even make a feint towards any explanation of what human rights are – that is a huge topic on its own. What must be noticed is that Bernie does not say that we have those rights as Americans, but as people. FDR did not go that far: he was proposing, not as a constitutional matter, but as part of our vision of ourselves as Americans, that we accept that we have economic rights as well as the political rights enshrined in the Constitution.

Bernie has not, so far as I know, proposed updating FDR's list of economic rights – however, that is something that he might well do someday.

In conclusion, if you look into it, neither FDR nor Bernie Sanders (nor any of the today's prominent democratic socialists) call for the wholesale change of the economy from private ownership to social ownership of dominant American industries. Their program is not that of (say) the socialist British Labor government in 1946 when it nationalized every major industry in the British economy as quickly as could be done. We must look at what Sanders and other democratic socialists advocate, not what they call themselves: they do not so much as hint at a Classical Socialist program.

If what they do propose is examined, it is clear that, despite calling themselves socialists, what is in fact being recommended in the here and now is what is nothing but programs that fall under the heading of their historical rivals, namely social democracy. What actually needs to be explained - I will turn to that later - is why in the world they call themselves socialists when they are actually social democrats? By so labelling themselves while proposing programs that are not at all socialist (classically speaking) they are causing much confusion in the public mind, especially to the right-wing defenders of capitalism.

Not only do none of today's democratic socialists act in the spirit of classical socialism and announce programs of nationalizing the core of the American economy, but you do not even find them recommending the nationalization of *any* industry in our economic system. They simply are not Classical Socialists, not even slimmed down versions of it - yet it is idea that they are, caused by talk of socialism, that terrifies critics. The advice is to look at what they propose not what name they give themselves.

It is time to look at some objections to those claims.

Bernie Sanders and Socialism (III)

Since Sanders is thought of as the arch-socialist in today's political world, after having looked at the major socialist organization in the U.S. today, I am spending some time looking at the major socialist political figure and trying to understand what he thinks democratic socialism is.

I have said that socialism will not turn up in the Democratic Party platform in the coming election. But surely, it will be objected, a piece of socialism may be there and Bernie is advocating just such a thing.

The argument is: Medicare for All is a piece of socialism; Bernie is advocating it and it is probable that the party platform will reflect some version of Medicare for All; hence both person and party are asking the American voting public to accept a socialist program.

Is Medicare for All, a single payer insurance system, socialist? Of course, if you mean, as Moscow Mitch does, that it is not capitalist, that it is not privately owned and operated to make profits for the owners, then it surely is a piece of socialism. But that only means it is a piece of anti-capitalism – and as we have seen that does not by itself earn the title of socialism.

I do not intend to say that Medicare for All is or that it isn't a socialist program – rather I want to remind you of a few facts.

What Bernie Sanders' call for Medicare for All amounts to is not Classical Socialism. Advocating Medicare for All is not one piece of a more general call to nationalize all major industries. Rather it is directed to one specific issue: to ensure the best way for all Americans to have access to health care. Even in its limited scope, it fails to be Classical Socialism: for neither Sanders, nor other Democrats, are recommending that all health insurance issuing entities be taken over and run by the government. For example, Blue Cross/Blue Shield investors and management will not be informed one day that the company is now owned by the United States and that management must now answer to the government and not the previous board of directors. Such a possibility has not ever crossed Sanders' mind nor that of other supporters of Medicare for All. So, if those who call it socialism vaguely have in mind what I have been calling Classical Socialism and hope that those who listen to their propaganda have such thoughts, then they need to be challenged.

On the other hand, one can easily fashion an argument that Medicare for All is socialism. Contrast it with Germany's classic social democratic solution to ensuring access to health care for Germans: there, health insurance is provided by private firms, very heavily regulated privately owned companies. Medicare for All is not at all like that: under it, health insurance would no longer be provided by privately owned companies. (I am ignoring here the fact that it is likely and desirable that supplemental policies might still be purchased by consumers from privately held companies even under a Medicare for All program.) Rather, insuring people's health care would be done by a branch of the federal government. Ownership of the existing health insurance corporations would not be transferred to the state – instead those companies would simply cease to be in that business (and perhaps some would cease to exist) and be replaced by a government agency whose function is to run a health insurance program for everyone. Thus, the aim of Medicare for All is to accomplish something of what Classical Socialism calls for: state operation of a major feature of our lives.

A second aim of the Classical Socialist program would also be involved in the creation of a Medicare for All scheme: the disappearance of profits arising from the issuing of health insurance policies. The government is not to make money from providing health insurance.

The upshot is that a Medicare for All program, while definitely part of the anti-capitalist project, would be both like and unlike socialism. Thus, there is no definitive answer as to whether it is or is not socialism. If we want to call it a socialist plan, or deny that it is, we need to realize that that is a matter of judgement. We might, in the end, go either way but the basic facts do not settle the issue.

It must also be kept in mind that Medicare for All is only about insurance – it does not so much hint at socializing health care – doctors, nurses, practitioners, hospitals, clinics, etc. The care itself will still be carried out by private normally capitalist (though some of them non-profit) enterprises.

One last item that inclines to the denial that Medicare for All is socialist. Earlier I pointed out that welfare programs do not fall solely into the socialist camp. Social democrats, who do not believe that capitalism should cease to be the basis of our economy, accept welfare programs as do socialists. Why? Because they are designed to help people to deal with human issues that are not entirely economic. Social Security is for people whose age (or physical condition) makes them not economic actors, not able to function in the economic system. What they need is welfare assistance. Access to health care is not a piece of our economic lives – it touches everyone, simply as people, whether they are currently participants in the economy or not.

It is thus possible to conceive Medicare for All not as a socialist endeavor, but part of a welfare scheme even within a quite robust capitalist economy. Health insurance is a major economic sector but is not a productive industry. That, for Classical Socialists, means that the health insurance industry is not to be socialized but treated as part of welfare – and social democrats can agree with that. Elizabeth Warren, who rightly denies being a socialist, is a hard-nosed defender of Medicare for All. (She, being a social democrat could have been advocating the German system. But, she argues, that the amount of money drained off from our health expenditures by private insurers is so great (profits, administrative costs), say $23 billion per year, money that could genuinely be spent on health care itself, that it is better to eliminate private insurance altogether.)

Bernie Sanders and Socialism (IV)

It has also been argued that Sanders', and potentially the Democratic Party's, plan to deal with climate change, global warming – call it The Green New Deal - is socialist.

To see whether it is or not, it is necessary to take some time to think about the issue of climate change.

Conservatives try to paint the Green New Deal – no matter which of the several variations – as proposed for socialist reasons, that it is an attempt to make our economy socialist. That is not so – the advocacy of the GND is not ideological. It is based on a claim that we (and the entire world) are facing a disaster in the not too far off future unless global warming is brought to a standstill. That claim is based on orthodox science – not at all a wild and wooly hypothesis. And that disaster, based also upon near unanimous scientific research, is being caused by our use of fossil fuels. Hence, the only way to save the earth and human life as we know it is by ending our use of fossil fuels.

And that is what the GND does: whatever other matters are included in variations on the main theme, it ends quickly the widespread use of fossil fuels.

Bernie Sanders (and AOC and the Sunrise Movement) are holding that climate change is like the emergency of World War II – and that what they propose can only be understood as a response to that emergency. Now if one wants to say they go too far, even in simply trying to halt climate change, that requires criticizing what the scientific community says: that we have only a short time to save ourselves and the earth.

That is, the GND is not introduced into American political discussion as an ideological matter. Rather it is held to be the solution to a disaster facing us. So, what is being proposed is not to be treated as a proposal for the institution of Socialism as an economic system.

Of course, there may be socialist provisions in whatever version of the GND you seize upon – but the entire program is not Socialist or Capitalist or whatever.

Now back to Bernie Sanders' version of it. He will argue that only his proposals are sufficient to accomplish what needs to be done: bringing global warming to a standstill. And are those proposals socialist in orientation?

Forget all the issues about timelines, about when such and such must be done. Those have to do with the scientific claims as well as technological and political realities, but they are not relevant to this discussion. And also forget about the issue of cost – that too is irrelevant here (though both irrelevancies are very important in assessing the overall Sanders' plan). What must be focused on is the core of the Sanders' solution, the stuff we might think of as socialist.

Most commentators say that there are two core principles to the plan and that these are what might be socialist. That is a too narrow view of the Sander's (and the Sunrise Movement's) versions of the GND. However, that correction of the standard media presentation of the proposal must wait for later. Right now, what is relevant are those two core elements – the aim will be to see whether they are genuine socialism.

The two elements have to do with energy and transportation. And the answer is, again, that they are and they are not socialist.

The Sanders' plan (as with other versions) would have all American electrical power generated from renewable sources, solar, wind, hydroelectric, geothermal. (He, arguably mistakenly, refuses to accept any type of nuclear power, i.e. using non-uranium fuel, as part of the solution.)

To achieve complete reliance on renewables, since there are not at present enough generating facilities to produce the needed amount of electrical power, the government will undertake to build what is needed (e.g. solar installations, wind farms...). These are the up-to-date variants on dams, which are government owned and generate electricity which is sold on the market. Thus, the proposed new types of government involvement in electricity generation involve no new political principles – they may still be thought of by the right as socialist, but there is no radical innovation in principle about what is to be done.

Sanders' proposal does not have the state taking over existing sources of renewable energy: the plan does not call for current renewable generation facilities to be nationalized. Nor is there anything in the plan, as far as I can tell, that requires only government produced electricity to be put into the grid. What is proposed is a (massive) supplement to existing arrangements. Of course, it may turn out that privately owned firms cannot compete in the long run and will wither away.

On the other hand, the socialist dream of not having profits generated by ownership would be satisfied by those new productive energy sources which are state owned.

Also, in the energy part of his GND, the Sanders' plan envisions a completely redone, federally owned, electrical grid, one that replaces the inefficient and outdated patchwork grid that we now have. Here, if you will, is a socialist project to replace the social democracy type of grid (privately owned but heavily regulated) we currently have.

As far as the transportation element of his plan, Bernie will be having only electrical vehicles of all sorts (including buses, trucks, etc.) produced and sold. The government will not be taking over vehicle production – production will still be done by Ford, Toyota, Volvo, etc. – but the current fossil fuel vehicles will not be allowed to be produced. There is no socialist takeover of transportation production: the form this piece of the climate solution proposal takes falls into the social democratic camp.

Lastly, with all the new vehicles being electric, what will be needed are sufficient and accessible charging stations. Clearly, gas stations will no longer be gas stations whatever they evolve into (and whenever since there will be a phaseout of current gasoline powered vehicles). And the plan does not, say, subsidize capitalist firms to build and own the vast new charging network (though private construction companies will no doubt be hired to do the installation). The charging stations will also be owned and operated by the government (by some government since there will be need for stations in municipalities) in just the same way that the Interstate Highway System (planned and built under conservative auspices) was.

In short, the GND proposed by the arch-socialist is a mixture of socialism, social democracy and capitalism. It is best simply to think of it as a piece of public investment done in a capitalist economy, just as was the Interstate Highway System.

Economic Democracy Afresh

Earlier I said that socialism cannot be understood except as an extension of democracy into the economic life of the country, that the entire purpose of having the state own and operate major economic actors is to enable economic democracy.

Perhaps I should have written this entire piece beginning with that theme. Sadly, I have adopted the conventional route and discussed the mechanism by which socialists try to achieve their purpose and have deferred until this late place any substantial discussion of that purpose.

Let me begin to examine what the socialists are up to by, astonishingly no doubt, looking at what major American capitalists have recently said.

Beginning about 1970, inspired by the University of Chicago economist Milton Friedman, American corporations have accepted the doctrine that the *only* aim of a corporation's activity is to make the most profit possible for its owners, its stockholders. It must not take anything else into consideration in making its plans. Since maximum profit is a corporation's sole aim, its executives must be judged, and consequently paid by taking into account nothing else but how well, under his (very rarely her) leadership, they have succeeded in achieving that aim. The CEO's pay will be delivered in the form of the company's stock and as the stock goes up, their compensation goes up: so they will do everything in their power to increase the price of the stock.

That is, the Friedman doctrine is a rejection of any idea that a corporation has any social responsibility over and above profit to its owners, its stockholders. That doctrine has led to a massive increase in the compensation of CEO's.

Given that American corporations have enthusiastically bought into the Friedman doctrine, it came as a great shock recently when a large number (181 to be exact) of the CEO's of major corporations (the Business Round Table) have, verbally at least, rejected it. In a new "Statement on the Purpose of a Corporation", those CEO's committed themselves to the idea that their corporations should be operated for the benefit of "all stakeholders". Who counts in their eyes as stakeholders? "Customers, employees, suppliers, communities and shareholders."

Now we mustn't think that those titans of industry have overnight become socialists at heart. They are not advocating the surrender of profits or the turning over of their companies to the state.

We must be deeply suspicious as to whether they shall even remotely begin to put into practice what they are now verbally committed to. Nonetheless, they are now talking the language of economic democracy. And that is a strong foot in the door for future socialist criticism of corporate behavior.

If we look at that list of stakeholders in a corporation (as seen by their CEO's), notice that there are two items missing there which would appear on a similar list drawn up by socialists today. First, there is no mention of the environment: those CEO's still have not seen that a corporation must take into account in its calculations and operations the world in which we live, the Earth, even more so today with global warming well underway. Today's socialists (see the DSA) would insist on that. Secondly, notice that there is no mention of workplace democracy: the statement agrees that a corporation must include in their calculations the well-being of its employees, but there is no recognition of a fact that today's socialists would insist upon, that democratic practices must be extended *into* the workplace, that workers need to play a major role in all manner of *decisions* concerning the operation of the corporation.

So, what the *Business Roundtable* advocates is a long way from what socialists want, but at the least they have accepted (at least in part) the economic democracy theme that is the background to socialist programs.

Let me switch now to a blurb from the DSA about what economic democracy is.

Today, corporate executives who answer only to themselves and a few wealthy stockholders make basic economic decisions affecting millions of people. Resources are used to make money for capitalists rather than to meet human needs. We believe that the workers and consumers who are affected by economic institutions should own and control them.

Social ownership could take many forms, such as worker-owned cooperatives or publicly owned enterprises managed by workers and consumer representatives.

Democratic socialists favor as much decentralization as possible. While the large concentrations of capital in industries such as energy and steel may necessitate some form of state ownership, many consumer-goods industries might be best run as cooperatives.

While much of that is familiar from what has been said earlier, I would like to call attention to two features of that material. First, notice that there are options for how industries, when not under capitalist control, could be owned. Social ownership of large industries, in contemporary democratic socialism, does not mean the operation will be managed by bureaucrats, by state functionaries: that is the standard interpretation of socialism by those who oppose it. However, socialism advocates, for the typical case, that though the enterprises are owned publicly, they will be "managed by workers and consumers". That is, those stakeholders will take the place of stockholders and boards of directors chosen by the stockholders. Of course, those stakeholders will, at least in most cases, hire professional managers to run the day to day business of the firm – that is, the CEO's etc. in socially owned firms will be beholden to the stakeholders not stockholders.

Secondly, notice that in this modern form of socialism, not all socialized enterprises need be owned by the state (and therefore the public). The importance of worker owned enterprises has grown in recent socialist theory: it has been realized that that kind of privately held firm is fully compatible with socialism. As long as the profit motive is absent and the interests of different kinds of stakeholders are not simply recognized but given a place at the table, worker co-operatives qualify as socialist. So, the old definition of socialism as *requiring* state ownership of significant corporations has been abandoned in recent socialist thought.

Including Economic Democracy in Practice

I pointed out much earlier that this country has, at different levels of government, publicly owned enterprises that have had a long history in our economic lives. In our mixed economy, there are socialist enterprises, from local fire departments to the Post Office to the TVA.

It is, however, important to realize that such common socialist agencies do not, largely at least, fully satisfy the socialist program. They are not privately owned for profit, but, on the whole, they are not run with economic democracy, the aim of socialism, in mind. They are simply publicly owned.

A true blue socialist might hold, in fact, that there is really no (or very little) socialism in American economic life – and that is because the aim of extending democracy into the economy has not yet been accomplished, even where the ownership is public not private.

That only the most obvious part of socialism, the holding of key features of the economy by the state, has been put into practice can be explained. Given the background that capitalism is so dominant in both our economic lives and our thinking and that for socialism to advance requires displacing such dominance, it is understandable that socialist efforts be directed toward getting a foot in the door, getting non-privately-owned enterprises a significant place in the economy. So, the failure to achieve the aim of socialism is understandable even if regrettable.

How far do the current proposals made by Bernie Sanders and others in the political arena aim at full economic democracy? If economic democracy is missing from those proposals, the strict socialist may well say that there are *no* socialist proposals being made by Democrats in the lead-up to the 2020 election.

Well, is there anything in our public discussions, in Democratic Party plans and platform, like what the British Labour Party in its recent (September 2019) conference proposed concerning worker participation? Labour proposed "sectoral bargaining for unions (through which unions would negotiate wage and working conditions for all the workers in an industry, regardless of union membership) ... giving workers a 10 percent share in the companies they work for, and requiring at least a third of company board of directors come from its workers." (from John Judis) There may be some of that in one or the other of Elizabeth Warren's plans – but such moves toward economic democracy is not a major element in any currently imagined Democratic Party program for 2020 and the immediate thereafter.

In short, the complete development of a socialist program in this country is not now a feature of the Democratic Party or its candidates.

And even the conventional basic feature of socialism, nationalizing major industries, is lacking in Democratic plans. Compare what the Labour Party in Britain has just called for: it "would also establish public ownership, with worker input, of railroads, utilities, including the electrical grid, and the mails." (John Judis) Nothing at all like that, except for the electrical grid, is proposed by any Democratic candidate for the Presidency or by anyone in a position to see that such a program is incorporated into the party platform for 2020. In short, the idea that the Democratic Party is now a socialist party is a complete fantasy of the right. Such misguided, even wild claims, are as usual like what the rooster crowing at break of day is up to: it is what the right does as a thoughtless reflex.

In Closing

I said at the beginning that I had no idea how many topics I might end up discussing. Well, I have the feeling that I shall stop here.

I do want to remind you of several further things.

This was not to be, and I hope is not, a scholarly effort. While it is intended for the intelligent reader, it is not intended for the academic world.

Secondly, it is intended to be useful for the 2020 elections. The Republicans have stated their aim to be to charge the Democratic candidate (and no doubt those running for other offices) with being socialists or at least in bed with socialists. That will be so no matter who the Democratic candidate is and no matter whether it is on the face of it true. That is overwhelmingly a propaganda claim – they show no ability to make proper discriminations between quite different ideological views. On the other hand, Democrats need to know the lessons of this pamphlet in order to respond to the inaccurate ideas of what socialism is. So, no matter what side of our current political divide you are on, this work will be of use.

The general conclusion that I have reached is that, given a proper understanding of what socialism is, there is, in the Democratic Party approaching the 2020 election, only a wee bit of socialism, of democratic socialism. It might even be unfortunate that there is not more: but the fact is that the Republican level of hysteria is so far out of touch with what the situation is we can only shake our heads in amazement.

When I started this project, I had hoped to be able to offer advice about how to respond to the charge of socialism. I have now largely abandoned the idea that

I can provide some specific guidance over and above what I have written here. Those who do want to object to the Republicans, will themselves have to adapt what I have said here to the local circumstances.

Lastly, remember that this is not a defense of socialism: it is an explanation of what it has been and is. What I have sympathy for is that we Americans, starting with the election at hand, need to examine and have reasonable discussions of proposals that we need to make substantial changes in our economic system: and the discussion of socialism needs to be one of the alternatives in that political study. Socialism may or may not be the most reasonable route for this country, but until we examine it – and capitalism as well – we will not be in a position to make the wise choice for how we ought to live economically.

Made in the USA
San Bernardino, CA
13 December 2019

61364529R00071